PIONEERS

PIONEERS

A LIBRARY OF CONGRESS BOOK

BY MARTIN W. SANDLER

Introduction by James Billington, Librarian of Congress

HarperCollins*Publishers*

This book is dedicated to the memory of Dr. Harvey J. Mendelsohn, a gentle giant whose kindness and compassion inspired young and old alike.

ACKNOWLEDGMENTS

The author wishes to thank Robert Dierker, senior advisor for multimedia activities of the Library of Congress, and Dana Pratt, director of publishing of the Library of Congress, for their encouragement and cooperation. Appreciation is expressed to Kate Murphy, Carol Weiss, Heather Henson, the staff of the Prints and Photographs Division of the Library of Congress, and Dennis Magnu of the Library's Photoduplication Service. A very special acknowledgment is made to the book's editor, Kate Morgan Jackson, whose dedication, skill and encouragement were invaluable to this project.

◆

Pioneers
A Library of Congress Book
Copyright © 1994 by Eagle Productions, Inc.

Library of Congress Cataloging-in-Publication Data
Sandler, Martin W.
Pioneers: a Library of Congress book / by Martin W. Sandler ; introduction by James H. Billington.
p. cm.
Summary: An overview, in text and illustrations, of the pioneer experience in the American West, from the first settlers through the development of towns.
ISBN 0-06-023023-1. — ISBN 0-06-023024-X (lib. bdg.)
1. Pioneers—West (U.S.)—Juvenile literature.   2. Pioneers—West (U.S.)—Pictorial works—Juvenile literature.   3. Frontier and pioneer life—West (U.S.)—Juvenile literature.   4. Frontier and pioneer life—West (U.S.)—Pictorial works—Juvenile literature.
[1. Pioneers—West (U.S.)   2. Frontier and pioneer life—West (U.S.)]   I. Title.
F596.S18   1994
978—dc20
92-47495
CIP
AC

Design by Tom Starace with Jennifer Goldman
1   2   3   4   5   6   7   8   9   10
❖
First Edition

Our type of democracy has depended upon and grown with knowledge gained through books and all the other various records of human memory and imagination. By their very nature, these records foster freedom and dignity. Historically they have been the companions of a responsible, democratic citizenry. They provide keys to the dynamism of our past and perhaps to our national competitiveness in the future. They link the record of yesterday with the possibilities of tomorrow.

One of our main purposes at the Library of Congress is to make the riches of the Library even more available to even wider circles of our multiethnic society. Thus we are proud to lend our name and resources to this series of children's books. We share Martin W. Sandler's goal of enriching our greatest natural resource—the minds and imaginations of our young people.

The scope and variety of Library of Congress print and visual materials contained in these books demonstrate that libraries are the starting places for the adventure of learning that can go on whatever one's vocation and location in life. They demonstrate that reading is an adventure like the one that is discovery itself. Being an American is not a patent of privilege but an invitation to adventure. We must go on discovering America.

James H. Billington
The Librarian of Congress

You are about to meet some of the most heroic figures in all of America's past. Their story represents one of the nation's greatest adventures—the settling of the great American West. It is a story larger than fiction, filled with real people with real dreams facing and overcoming enormous challenges. Above all, it is the story of men, women and children who made the pioneering spirit a vital part of the American character.

MARTIN W. SANDLER

WESTWARD HO!

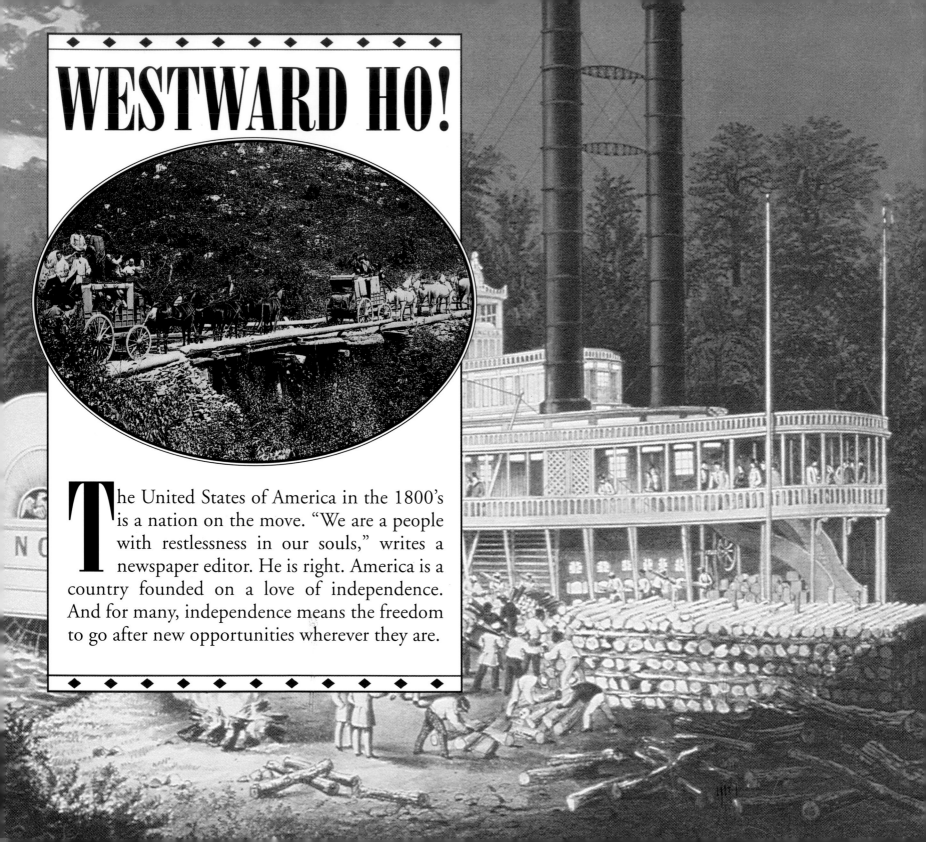

The United States of America in the 1800's is a nation on the move. "We are a people with restlessness in our souls," writes a newspaper editor. He is right. America is a country founded on a love of independence. And for many, independence means the freedom to go after new opportunities wherever they are.

For millions of Americans, the greatest opportunities lie in the vast lands of the West. Into these lands pour hunters and farmers, artists and adventurers, missionaries and shopkeepers. Some hope to strike it rich. Most want to build a new life for themselves and their families. They will include some of the most romantic figures the nation has ever known— mountain men, gold seekers, lumberjacks, and cowboys. They are all pioneers. They will carve a new nation out of the wilderness.

FALLING
CREW
No 1225

It will not be easy. The long journey to the West will test the courage and determination of all who attempt it. Once there, the pioneers will encounter a whole new set of hardships and dangers. Out of their great adventure will emerge a simple fact: The great heroes of the West will not be larger-than-life figures like the cowboy or the lumberjack. They will be the pioneer farmer and the pioneer family.

The real story of the American frontier will tell of ordinary people struggling to work the land and build new lives. They will face many dangers and disappointments, but they will succeed. The crops they raise will cover the prairie. They will see towns and cities rise. They will feed the nation and much of the world.

In the early 1800's, most Americans live in cities, towns and farms along the East Coast. But there is a special group of men who live and work in the mountains well beyond the settled areas of the East. They are hunters and trappers, and they play an essential part in the giant fur industry. These mountain men, as they are called, will play a key role in the settlement of the West.

[There is] no class of men on the face of the earth who lead a life of more continued exertion, peril, and excitement . . . than the free trappers of the West. . . . [Let] but a single track of beaver meet his eye and he forgets all dangers and defies all difficulties.

—Washington Irving,
A Tour on the Prairies, 1835

The mountain man's equipment includes his rifle, shot and powder; his traps; a hunting knife and a hatchet. His greatest treasure is his horse.

Chasing their main target, the beaver, takes the hunters and trappers through and over the mountains and across the Great Plains, which are filled with streams where the beavers live. It is a hard life. The mountain men live off the land and face danger at every turn. Winters bring bitter cold and fierce snowstorms. Accidents are common. And there is always the threat of attack from a bear or other wild animal that is not about to give up its fur and its life without a fight.

The hunters and trappers are among the first white men to enter the vast lands known as the Great Plains. There they meet the Native Americans who have lived on the Plains for thousands of years. There aren't many hunters and trappers, and most of these Native Americans do not feel threatened by them. While the mountain men approach each new group of Native Americans cautiously, most develop peaceful relations with these people who have lived on the Plains long before the first white people appeared.

The Native Americans of the Plains become an important part of the American fur trade. Many are skilled and courageous hunters, and in exchange for blankets, guns, beads and whiskey, they supply the mountain men with furs of every type and with the hides of buffalo, deer and elk.

In time, the mountain men become more than just hunters and trappers. Because they know the mountain regions so well, the government hires some of them to blaze trails through those areas. These early trails help restless easterners to move westward. The mountain men also find new jobs as guides and scouts for these adventurous early pioneers. Over the years, tales of their courage and daring are spread through story and song. Men like Daniel Boone and Kit Carson become legendary figures.

I can't say as ever I was lost, but I was <u>bewildered</u> once for three days.
—Daniel Boone,
response to a question asked by
his portrait painter, 1819

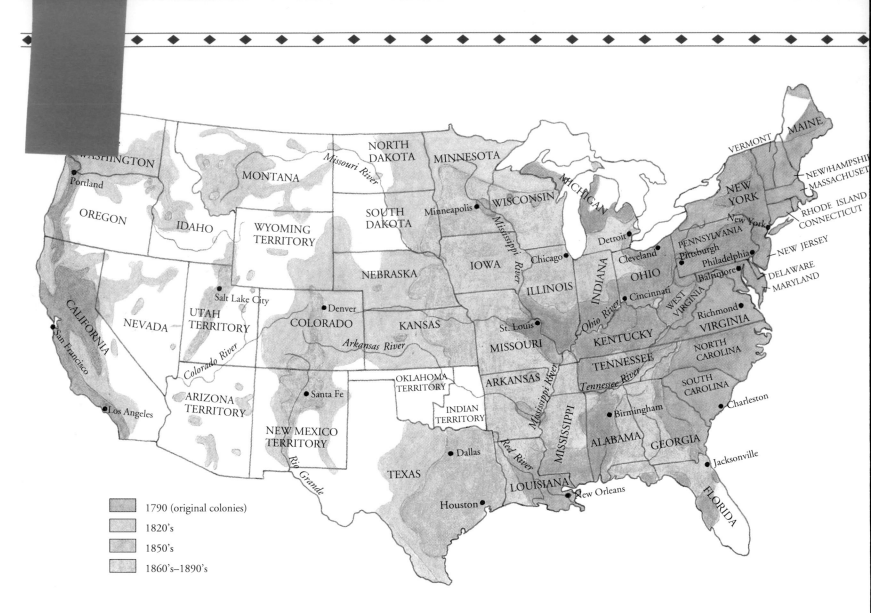

1790 (original colonies)

1820's

1850's

1860's–1890's

The men, women and children who follow the trailblazers through the mountain passes will be the first to push the American frontier westward. This first wave of pioneers will settle in the western wilderness areas of established eastern states and in the western wilds of territories such as Kentucky, Tennessee and Ohio. By the 1840's, pioneers will push the frontier westward beyond the Mississippi River. Between the 1850's and the 1890's, the largest of all the waves of pioneers will extend the frontier thousands of miles across the Great Plains, all the way to the Pacific Ocean.

The land between the eastern mountains and the Mississippi River is covered with millions of trees. The forests are so thick, it is said, that a squirrel could spend its entire life moving from tree to tree without ever touching the earth. The early frontier family's first job is to clear enough land to build a house and plant its first crops.

Clearing the forest is hard work, but the trees are a blessing. The settlers cut them into logs to build their homes. They keep themselves warm in winter by burning wood from the endless supply that surrounds them. The roots and stumps from the felled trees, along with the rocky soil, make farming difficult, but the woods are filled with wildlife, and the settlers become excellent hunters. Much of the food they eat comes from the animals they track down in the forests.

At <u>cutting down</u> trees or <u>cutting them up</u>, the Americans will do <u>ten times</u> as much in a day as any other men I ever saw. Let one of these men on upon a wood of timber trees, and his slaughter will astonish you.

—1820's British editor

By the 1840's, American magazines back East feature illustrations of people who have successfully moved into the frontier areas. The early settlers become an inspiration for those who follow them. Yet, for many of these early pioneers, the adventure has just begun. Their restlessness will cause thousands of them to look for more land, richer soil and even greater opportunities much farther to the west.

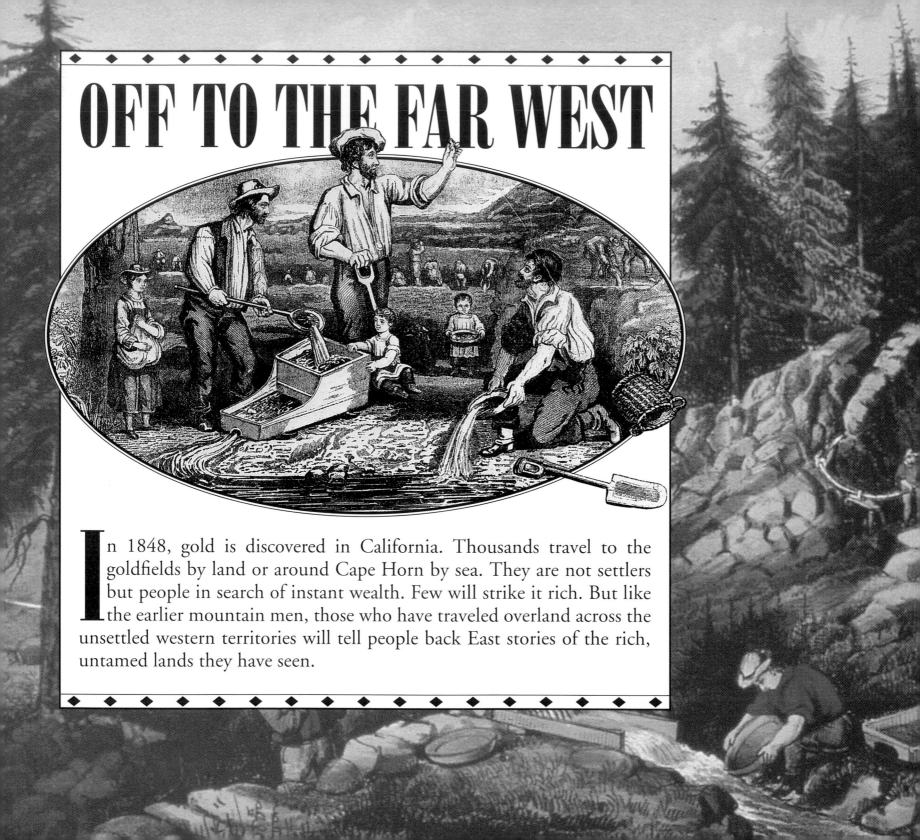

OFF TO THE FAR WEST

In 1848, gold is discovered in California. Thousands travel to the goldfields by land or around Cape Horn by sea. They are not settlers but people in search of instant wealth. Few will strike it rich. But like the earlier mountain men, those who have traveled overland across the unsettled western territories will tell people back East stories of the rich, untamed lands they have seen.

The California gold strike is the first of several strikes that take place in the 1800's. The Nevada, Colorado, Montana and Dakota territories all experience gold rushes. In the late 1800's, gold is discovered in the Klondike region of Alaska. More than 100,000 gold seekers climb the steep, icy trails in search of instant wealth. The Klondike adventure becomes a symbol of how much people will risk and how far they will travel in search of opportunity.

When they return East, the gold miners tell stories of millions of animals grazing wild on the prairie lands. They speak of scenery beautiful beyond description. Most often they talk of open spaces that stretch farther than the eye can see, spaces waiting to be settled. Many back East don't believe these tales. But soon there are pictures that offer proof.

Adventurous artists travel to the far western lands and bring the stories to life with their paints and brushes.

During their travels, the artists encounter the Native Americans of the Great Plains. Men like Karl Bodmer and George Catlin begin to paint scenes of the Native Americans and their way of life. They do so at a time before the first Native Americans are driven from the Plains by overpowering numbers of whites. The paintings reveal people living close to nature amidst beautiful surroundings, people with a strong sense of family unity.

Crumbo

The Native Americans of the Plains are a deeply spiritual people. They believe that higher powers rule over everything they do. Their various dances, their dress and their ceremonies are designed to maintain harmony with nature.

In 1839, the miracle of photography is announced. In the decades that follow, photographers such as William Henry Jackson and Timothy O'Sullivan join the early artists in the West. They lug their glass-plate negatives and bulky equipment across the land and to the tops of the western mountains. They capture spectacular scenes and send their pictures back East. The photographs are quickly purchased by a public increasingly eager for pictures of the lands they are beginning to hear so much about.

An examination of these pictures fills us with admiration and amazement. Admiration for this magnificent scenery of our own country, which is scarcely excelled by that of any other. . . . Amazement that such work could be executed in the wild regions of the Rocky Mountains.

—Philadelphia photographer, c.1870

LEAVING FOR A NEW LAND

Tens of thousands of Americans are eager for new opportunities. New England farmers are tired of trying to make a living on their rocky native soil. Other men and women are anxious for new adventures. But the great majority of people looking for new horizons live in the rapidly growing cities. In the years ahead, the cities will become even more crowded as millions of immigrants from countries throughout Europe pour into them seeking a new life in a new world. Thousands of these immigrants will eventually join the ranks of other city dwellers who head West.

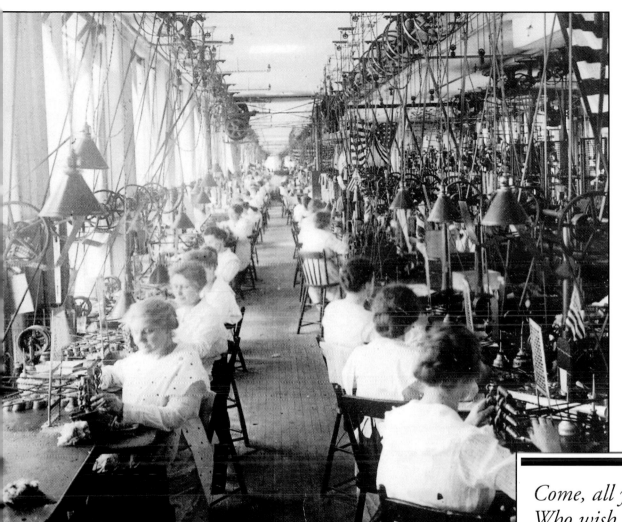

housands of these city dwellers work in the factories. Factory work is hard, the hours are long and the pay is low. Most families are so poor that their children are forced to work as well. Boys and girls as young as ten years old operate dangerous machinery from dawn to dusk. Many poor families are especially willing to risk everything for a new chance in a new land.

Come, all ye sons of labor
Who wish to change your lot,
Who've spunk enough to travel
Beyond your native cot;
Come, leave the crowded cities
Where work is overdone,
And come with us to settle
In western Kansas towns.

—From "Immigration Song"

Every month seems to bring announcements of new lands now open for settlement, but the pioneers' gain is the Native Americans' loss. Almost all of the new territory has been taken from the Native Americans through force and broken treaties.

GRAND RUSH
FOR THE
INDIAN
TERRITORY!
Over 15,000,000 Acres of Land
NOW OPEN FOR SETTLEMENT!
Being part of the Land bought by the Government in
1866 from the Indians for the Freedmen.

NOW IS THE CHANCE
TO
PROCURE A HOME
In this Beautiful Country!

THE FINEST TIMBER!
THE RICHEST LAND!
THE FINEST WATERED!
WEST OF THE MISSISSIPPI RIVER.

Every person over 21 years of age is entitled to 160 acres, either by pre-emption or homestead, who wishes to settle in the Indian Territory. It is estimated that over Fifty Thousand will move to this Territory in the next ninety days. The Indians are rejoicing to have the whites settle up this country.

The Grand Expedition will Leave Independence May 7, 1879

Independence is situated at the terminus of the Kansas City, Lawrence & Southern Railroad. The citizens of Independence have laid out and made a splendid road to these lands; and they are prepared to furnish emigrants with complete outfits, such as wagons, agricultural implements, dry goods, groceries, lumber and such. They have also opened an office there for general information to those wishing to go to the Territory. IT COSTS NOTHING TO BECOME A MEMBER OF THIS COLONY.
Persons passing through Kansas City will apply at the office of K. C. L. & S. R. R. opposite Union Depot, for Tickets.

ABOUT THE LANDS.

As 1850 approaches, the United States government begins to open various western territories to settlement. Countless Americans are ready to move to the new lands. Soon the government offers an even greater reward: It will give 160 acres of land (a quarter of a square mile), free of charge, to any family that settles that land, improves it and lives on it for at least five years. Men, women and children take to the road. They travel on foot, by handcart and in covered wagons. The rush to the West has begun.

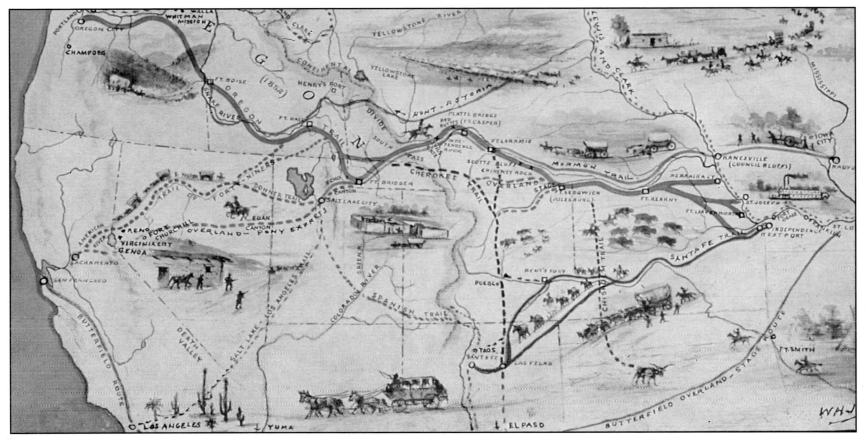

There are several routes that the pioneers can take to the West. None are easy. The most popular is the Oregon Trail, which is really nothing more than a pair of ruts cut into the earth by the thousands of wagons moving west. The Oregon Trail runs for 2,400 miles across the endless grasslands of the prairies, through the enormous desert beyond and over the treacherous Rocky Mountains. All the major trails—the Oregon, the Santa Fe and others—begin at one of the early, rough frontier towns along the Missouri River. At "jumping-off places" in Missouri such as Independence, St. Joseph or Kansas City, pioneer families gather, join up with a wagon train and begin the most difficult journey of their lives.

If hell lay to the west, Americans would cross heaven to reach it.
—Early 1800's American proverb

We cross the prairies as of old
The pilgrims crossed the sea,
To make the West,
as they, the East,
The homestead of the free.

—From song, "The Kansas Emigrant"

As the pioneers make their way toward their new homes, the thousands of wagons that carry them and their possessions become symbols of their great adventure. The cloth tops of the wagons waving in the wind make each wagon train look like a fleet of ships. These wagons are given a name. They are called prairie schooners, or "ships of the plains." The "schooners" will be on the trail for as many as 150 days. Every step of the way will be filled with hardship.

Cover

Bows

Brake

Wagon Bed

Jockey Box

Grease Bucket

Tongue

Iron Tire

FLOUR

SEED

Space within a covered wagon is limited, so each family must carefully consider what to take and what to leave behind. Packing enough food and water for the long journey is, of course, a necessity. Tools are vital as well. Things like seed, candles, household utensils, guns and ammunition cannot be forgotten. But life is made up of more than necessities. Mother cannot imagine starting life in a strange place without her favorite dishes, books or family pictures. Father has his special chair. The children are determined to take their favorite toys. Sadly, for countless pioneer families these treasures will be the first items left along the trail as wagons begin to break down under the heavy load.

[Long] wings of white canvas stretch away on either side. . . . Myriads of horses and mules drag on the moving mass of humanity toward the setting sun.

—Member of a wagon train, 1864

They may be called "schooners," but the wagons are not built for water travel. The trail is filled with many rivers and streams that must be crossed. Animals balk without firm earth beneath their feet. Shifting currents and drifting logs make crossing even the calmest-looking river an adventure. The crudely marked graves on the banks of many rivers and streams serve as a grim reminder that moving west is a dangerous experience.

Delay is the greatest enemy. The pioneers set out in the spring so they can reach the West before the bitter winter snows set in. But delays cannot be avoided. Axles break, wheels fall off and the wagon train must stop while repairs are made. When the wagon train stops, some children get lost amidst the hundreds of families and animals. Others stray into the tall prairie grass and can't find their way back. None of the trails is marked, and precious time is lost looking for shortcuts by following cutoffs that lead to nowhere.

angers and hardships increase as the pioneers travel farther west. Countless children and adults are injured or even killed when wagons tip over while crossing the rocky areas that lie at the foot of the mountains. Illness takes a terrible toll. There are no doctors or hospitals along the way, and many die from lack of medical attention. The delays mount up, and before their journey is over many families are forced to make their way through treacherous mountain passes blocked by the snows they so desperately wished to avoid.

Thoughts stray back to the comfortable homes we left behind and the question arises, is this a good move? The wagon train is divided, some want to turn back; others favor going on. A decision is reached at noon; the train is to move on.

—Diary of a pioneer woman, 1849

From the moment they set
out, pioneer families are
frightened by stories of Indians attacking the wagons.
But most of these stories are false.
Few pioneers realize that it is a
custom among many tribes to exchange gifts with strangers. Those
pioneers who understand this custom are rewarded with badly
needed fresh meat and fish, which
they trade for goods stored in the
wagons.

Some rare but deadly attacks do take place. They
are launched by bands of Native Americans determined to drive the pioneers out of the land
that has been their home for thousands of years.
Says one chief, "When we saw the plows in the wagons, we knew these strangers meant to stay. And we
knew things would never be the same."

Above everything else, the pioneers are determined and courageous people. They have risked everything to build a new life for themselves and their children. Despite all the hardships, despite the fact that many have died and others have turned back along the way, the vast majority complete their journey. They still face many uncertainties in a strange land thousands of miles from the homes they left behind. But their ordeals on the trail have strengthened them for whatever lies ahead.

I can hardly describe my feelings on reaching here. The place so long desired to see. I could hardly believe that the long journey was accomplished and I had found a home.

—Diary of a pioneer woman, 1851

BY STAGECOACH, BOAT AND TRAIN

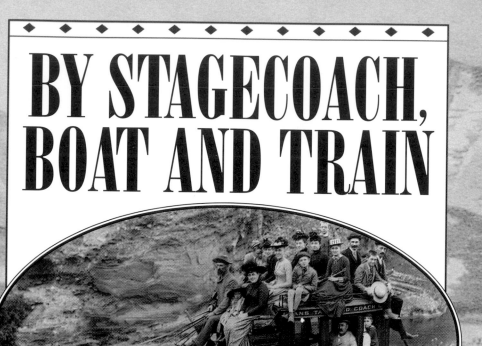

Covered wagons are not the only vehicles that begin to fill the West. As trails get better and roads are built, those who can afford it make the journey by stagecoach. The coaches, pulled by teams of six horses, travel day and night. Tired horses are exchanged for fresh ones at "home stations," which are built along the route.

For many pioneers, the overland trails seem too difficult to face, so they choose to make much of their journey over water. The vast network of great American rivers, including the Ohio, the Mississippi and the Missouri, leads to New Orleans in one direction and to the Great Plains in another. The flatboats that travel these rivers bring passengers and goods to new lands and new opportunities.

Before long there is a more modern way to travel by water. The western migration takes place at a time when a great age of American invention is beginning. One of the most dramatic of these developments is the harnessing of steam energy. Soon steamships dominate the docks of such river ports as Memphis, Cincinnati and St. Louis.

The steamboat is an ideal vessel for America. The nation is filled with countless rivers and waterways. Millions of trees that grow along the riverbanks supply the fuel for the vessels. For a people on the move, the steamboat is an invention that could not have come at a better time.

The invention of the steamboat was intended for us. The puny rivers of the East are only as creeks, or convenient waters on which experiments may be made for our advantage.

—*Cincinnati Gazette,* early 1800's

ut there is another, even more dramatic, invention. In the 1820's, the train begins to make its appearance. By 1835, over a thousand miles of track are laid throughout the East. To early Americans, the locomotive is as magical as a spaceship would be. It will play the most important role of all in the settling of the West.

lmost from the moment it is invented, there are those who realize that the train can be the perfect vehicle to carry pioneers to the West. In 1862, President Abraham Lincoln signs a law calling for the building of a railroad that will cross the nation. Within a year, the prairie begins to be covered with the wooden ties upon which the tracks will be laid.

Building the transcontinental railroad is an enormous task. Tunnels are blasted through mountains. Bridges are constructed over rivers. Snow-sheds are erected to protect trains, tracks and workers. Thousands of laborers are brought in from as far away as China and Ireland. It takes over six years, but in 1869 the job is completed. East and West are united by two bands of steel.

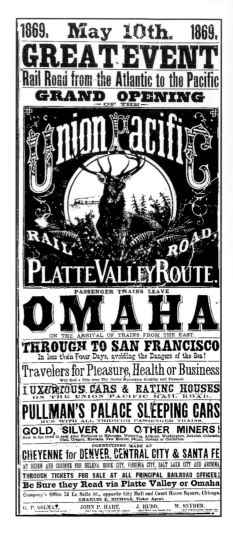

The great Pacific Railway,
For California hail!
Bring on the locomotive;
Lay down the iron rail.

—From song, "The Railroad Cars
Are Coming"

Less than a week after its completion, the transcontinental railroad is open to passengers. It is a transportation miracle. The five-month overland journey across the continent is reduced to eight days by rail. By the 1880's, travelers can choose from four more transcontinental lines that now span the nation.

By the end of the 1800's, the train is as common to the West as the buffalo and the prairie fire. Railroad companies, anxious to attract customers, buy up huge amounts of western lands and offer them for sale to would-be settlers. Between 1870 and 1890 millions of people travel to the West by train.

Only an emigrant bound
*   westward, ho!*
Only an emigrant,
*   then let me go;*
Longing to settle
*   'neath Liberty's dome!*
Only an emigrant
*   seeking a home . . .*
Willing for anything
*   honest I be*
Surely there's room on the
*   prairie for me. . . .*
            —From "Emigrant Song"

PRODUCTS WILL PAY FOR LAND AND IMPROVEMENTS!

MILLIONS OF ACRES

View on the Big Blue, between Camden and Crete, representing Valley and Rolling Prairie Land in Nebraska.

A SECTIONAL MAP, showing exact location of our IOWA LANDS is sold for 30 Cents, and of NEBRASKA LANDS for 30 Cents.

CIRCULARS are supplied GRATIS for distribution in ORGANIZING COLONIES and to induce individuals to emigrate WEST.

IOWA AND NEBRASKA LANDS

FOR SALE ON 10 YEARS CREDIT

BY THE

Burlington & Missouri River R.R. Co.

AT 6 PER CT. INTEREST AND LOW PRICES.

Only One-Seventh of Principal Due Annually, beginning Four Years after purchase.

20 PER CENT. DEDUCTED FROM 10 YEARS PRICE, FOR CASH.

LAND EXPLORING TICKETS SOLD

and Cost allowed in First Interest paid, on Land bought in 30 days from date of ticket.
Thus our Land Buyers GET A FREE PASS *in the State where the Land bought is located.*
These TERMS are BETTER at $5, than to pre-empt United States Land at $2.50 per Acre.
EXTRAORDINARY INDUCEMENTS on FREIGHT and PASSAGE are AFFORDED TO PURCHASERS and THEIR FAMILIES.

Address GEO. S. HARRIS, LAND COMMISSIONER,
or T. H. LEAVITT, Ass't Land Comm'r, Burlington, Iowa.

Or apply to

FREE ROOMS for buyers to board themselves are provided at Burlington and Lincoln.

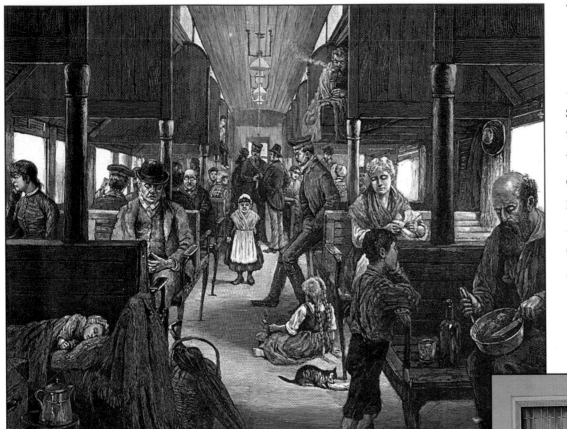

Despite what the railroad posters claim, most of these trains are hardly luxurious. Passengers sit on straight-backed wooden seats. Hot cinders and smoke from the wood-burning steam engine often pour in through the open windows. Along the way, the train makes frequent stops at hastily built, crude railway stations. There are no dining cars to make the journey more pleasurable. But it is the fastest way to travel yet invented, and soon the train is known as "the modern ship of the plains."

For thousands of European immigrants, the train trip to the West is the last stage of a long journey. Their travels have already taken them across the Atlantic Ocean to eastern city ports. Now, as they wait to board the train, their faces reflect their concern over traveling into the unknown.

The great American poet Walt Whitman describes the train as "emblem of motion and power, pulse of the continent." The railroad changes the face of the West. Farmers' crops will be shipped back East over the rails. Goods of every type will be transported from eastern cities to the remotest western areas. Businesses will grow wherever the train stops. Towns, and eventually cities, will spring up along the tracks.

THE AMERICAN COWBOY

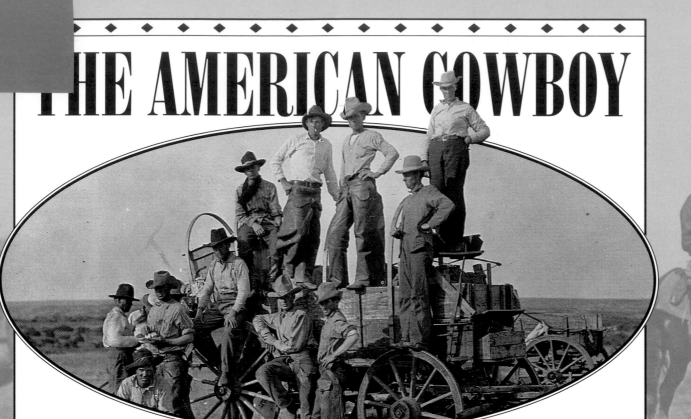

Many of the young men who travel to the West are not interested in becoming settlers; they want to be cowboys. By 1885, almost 1,400,000 square miles—44 percent of the land in the United States—is devoted to raising cattle. Forty thousand cowboys tend these cattle and drive them hundreds of miles over the open range to market. Most of the cowpunchers are in their twenties. Some are women, and are called cowgirls. And more than 5,000 of the cattlemen are African-American. Before he passes into history, the cowboy will become one of the most celebrated of all Americans, the subject of countless songs, movies and television programs.

Everything a cowboy wears has a purpose. His leather chaps protect his legs and trousers from the prickly underbrush. His wide-brimmed hat protects him from the sun, wind and rain. The pointed toes on his boots help him feel for the stirrups, while his high heels give him a firm footing when he is on the ground bringing a roped calf to a halt. His most valuable piece of equipment is his saddle. Types of saddle vary, but all have a high horn in front, to which the cowboy attaches his rope after lassoing a steer.

The cowboy has a tough job to do. Stampeding cattle, bucking broncos and long days battling the elements of nature are all part of his life. But he is happy to be where he is. Love of the outdoor life, a fierce spirit of independence and an admiration for the animals that surround him are the qualities that mark the American cowboy.

This was the way to live. . . . A body got so's he felt everything was kin to him, the earth and sky and buffalo and beaver and the yellow moon at night. It was better than being walled in by a house, better than breathing in spoiled air and feeling caged like a varmint.
—A. B. Guthrie, Jr., *The Big Sky*, 1947

The spring roundup, which can last for more than a month, is one of the main events in the cowboy's life. Cowboys ride for hundreds of miles, collecting cows from the open range. They rope and separate the calves to be branded from the older cattle, which will be driven to market. Cowboys from neighboring ranches often join together to collect all the cattle from a particular district. At the end of a roundup, hundreds of cowboys from different ranches join for a rare social gathering.

1877 A ROUND UP 1887

Branding cattle requires great skill. First a cowboy cuts a young cow from the herd. Then he ropes it and stops it long enough for two other cowhands to toss ropes around the animal's rear legs. Once the cow is on the ground, it is held down and branded with a hot iron carrying a distinctive mark that will let everyone know to which ranch the animal belongs.

Between the late 1860's and the late 1890's, cowboys drive more than nine million head of cattle to markets in Kansas. There the cattle are loaded on railroad cars and shipped east to slaughter-houses in Kansas City or Chicago. A typical cattle drive involves two or three thousand longhorn steer, sixty or seventy horses and ten or twelve cowboys. A trail boss heads the drive. The most experienced cowboys ride at the front and side of the herd while the youngest cowhands, called wranglers, bring up the dust-filled rear. During the drive, which can last up to five or six months, the cowboys are in the saddle almost eighteen hours a day.

The cowboys are great storytellers. Many of the myths that grow up about them come from the songs they sing and the tall tales they tell about themselves. Their real story is heroic enough, but their days are numbered. As the railroads reach out into every area of the West, cowboys no longer need to drive cattle to far-off railroad yards. As the number of western settlers increases, much of the open range will be fenced in. However, like the mountain men before them, the cowboys remind us of a time when men and women in love with freedom could live as they chose in the midst of nature.

Just as the cowboy arises out of the nation's need for meat, another frontier figure emerges out of the country's demand for huge amounts of wood. Into the huge forests of territories such as Michigan, Wisconsin and Oregon come men armed with axes, wedges and saws. They cut down the trees, saw them into logs and haul the logs to rivers, where they are floated to the sawmills. In an age of little understanding of the need to conserve resources, the lumberjacks wipe out entire forests. The lumber they produce will build the homes, towns and cities of America.

THE FRONTIER FAMILY

The cowboy and the lumberjack leave their mark on the American West. But the frontier farmers make the most important contribution. These pioneers introduce families into the West. They build homes and work the land. They are there to stay.

The farm families' first homes are nothing like those in the guide-books. Some families live in dugouts cut into the side of a hill. Most build their homes out of the prairie earth. This sod is so thick, it can be cut into strips and used the way bricks are used to build a house. Cracks are filled with clay and dirt, while the roof is covered with brush or hay. The soddies, as they are called, are cramped and leak terribly in the rain. But they are cool in summer and warm in winter. They provide the families with needed shelter while they get their all-important first crops into the ground.

My house it is built of the national soil,
The walls are erected according to Hoyle,
The roof has no pitch but is level and plain
And I always get wet when it happens to rain.
—From song, "The Lane County Bachelor"

The prairie soil is incredibly rich. As the earth is first turned over, the farmers are aided by a new and simple invention, a steel plow perfected by a Vermont farm boy named John Deere. The plow digs deep into the earth and is perfect for cutting into the dense, root-matted prairie soil.

Pioneer farming is a true family venture. The labor of everyone—father, mother, grandparents, children—is needed. The main crops are wheat, corn, alfalfa, potatoes, barley and oats. And there are horses, cows, pigs, sheep and chickens to raise and look after. The chores are many, the hours are long and there is little time for play.

Pioneer families are large, with as many as six to twelve children. The youngsters are vital to the family's survival. Small children feed the chickens, gather the eggs and pick wild nuts, berries and fruits. They search the largely treeless prairie for anything that can be burned as fuel—twigs, dried corncobs, flower stalks and, most important, dried cow and buffalo manure. Their older brothers and sisters plow and plant, pitch hay, haul water from the well and tend to the animals. Boys and girls of every age are expected to help with the laundry and kitchen chores.

The high point of the farmers' year is the harvest. The abundant crops must be picked and stored before they spoil in the field. Everyone is involved in the harvesting operations. Fathers and mothers, sons and daughters work from sunup to sundown, breaking only for a quick lunch in the field. They all wear some type of hat or bonnet to protect themselves from the scorching sun. When each day's harvesting is done, there are still the animals to feed, the fences to be mended and the countless other household and farm chores to be completed.

At this moment every man and boy, and even women, are actively engaged in [gathering] the golden harvest. . . . There is not help enough in the country to secure the crop.

—South Michigan pioneer farmer, 1839

The hours are long and the work seems never ending. But there are real benefits as well. Relationships within a pioneer farm family are close. Each member relies on the others. For perhaps the last time in American life, boys and girls get to see what their parents do and work alongside them.

There are many hardships for the pioneer family. Winter blizzards fill the plains with mountains of snow. The summer brings long stretches of terribly hot, dry weather. Water becomes scarce as wells and streams dry up. In extreme droughts, the prairie soil turns to dust. Fierce winds bring dangerous dust storms, the worst of which force families to flee from the land.

The dust clouds float upon the breeze
Through drooping corn and
*   wilting trees.*
The wheat fields all are
*   lifeless brown;*
The sunflower leaves
*   hang limping down.*
                    —From song, "Greer County"

The droughts bring another terror to families who have worked so hard to raise their crops. Each fall, as the tall prairie grass grows drier and drier, lightning or a carelessly tended campfire can cause a prairie fire. It is a terrifying and devastating experience. Walls of flame, almost impossible to control, jump from field to field. In a matter of minutes the results of a family's long labors can be turned into ashes.

As if fire and drought are not enough, hordes of grasshoppers periodically invade the grasslands. If they are not stopped, they can eat their way through entire fields of wheat, corn or alfalfa. Families must quickly gather infected grass and crops and burn them before the insects can spread throughout the farm.

The setbacks caused by nature are serious. But there is also another kind of hardship. The pioneer family's nearest neighbors are often as many as thirty miles away. The empty prairie beyond the fields seems to stretch forever, and the wind constantly howls a mournful tune. Loneliness is perhaps the greatest hardship of all.

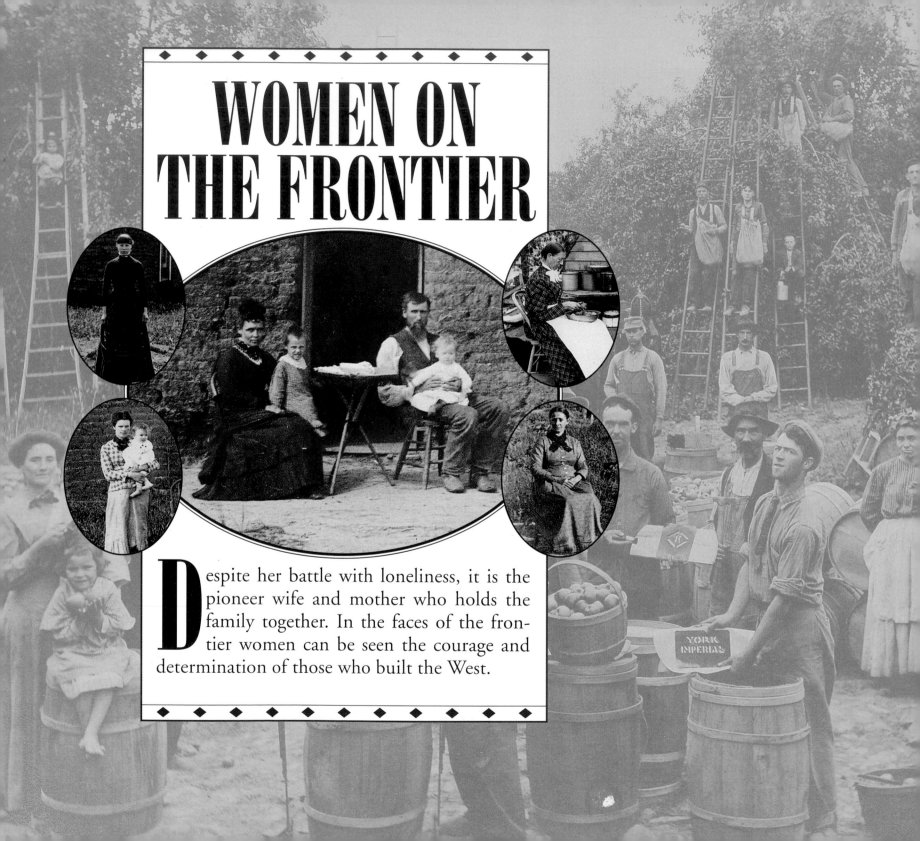

WOMEN ON THE FRONTIER

Despite her battle with loneliness, it is the pioneer wife and mother who holds the family together. In the faces of the frontier women can be seen the courage and determination of those who built the West.

The long journey to the West tests the bravery of every woman who makes the trip. Many have reluctantly uprooted themselves and their children because their husbands are determined to go. Yet once on the trail, most of the women find a courage they did not know they possessed. They are full partners with their husbands in a dangerous adventure.

Once she arrives on her new land, the pioneer woman finds that the tests of her spirit and strength are only beginning. Her labor will often be required in the field. But she will also have to spend long hours cooking, canning, preserving meat and making all of her family's clothing, all without any plumbing or electricity.

Thousands of pioneers are widowed or unmarried single women. They build their homes and farm their land without the help of husband or children. Their independent spirit is an important part of the story of what women accomplish in the West.

She is mother, wife, nurse, cook, doctor, comforter, teacher and farm laborer. Largely through her efforts and urging, clcancr and bcttcr homes will be erected, religion will be maintained and schools will be built. She will be regarded as a true heroine, and she will earn a proud nickname—the Madonna of the Plains.

O you daughters of the West
O you young and elder daughters!
O you mothers and you wives!
Never must you be divided, in our ranks you move united,
Pioneers! O Pioneers!
—"Pioneers, O Pioneers," Walt Whitman

THE MIRACLE OF MACHINERY

I t is a hard life, this pioneer farming. But by the late 1870's, it begins to change dramatically. New farming machines begin to make the pioneer farm family's life easier and more productive than anyone could have ever imagined it would be. Soon machinery will change every phase of the farm operation.

Before machinery, even the most efficient pioneer farm families have to limit the number of acres they plant. One family simply cannot harvest huge crops by hand before the produce spoils in the field. Farm machinery changes all that. The same farmer who in the 1860's was forced to limit the wheat crop to about 7 acres can, by the late 1870's, devote more than 135 acres to it.

The saucy machine has driven the scythe from the field . . . and the principal work of harvest, now, is to drive the horse about the field a few times and lo!, the harvest is gathered.

—1850's newspaper editor

Farm machinery inventions continue and soon one of the most important developments of all takes place. Ways are found to produce steam-driven tractors. These huge machines can pull the heaviest new farm equipment. They can haul the mechanical plows, reapers, threshers, combines and binders far faster than the best and largest horse teams ever assembled could. The prairie, so recently dominated by horses, is now filled with the new steel-plated, smoke-belching marvels of the age.

efore the 1800's are over, the pioneer farm families, who once struggled to plow or harvest 2 acres a day, will be able to plow or harvest more than 100. Thanks to machinery, they will be able to produce and sell far more crops and animals, and they will be able to do so in less time and with fewer hands than before. For the first time since answering the challenges of the West, pioneer farm families will actually have some time to enjoy the fruits of their labor.

FUN ON THE FRONTIER

Even though they work long hours, most pioneer families have managed to find a bit of time for fun. Children hitch rides on the hay wagon, climb trees, and seek out swimming holes and streams in the summer. Picnics and card playing are popular family pastimes. There are also games such as croquet, billiards and bowling. As the use of farm machinery reduces working hours, pioneer families begin to find more opportunities for pleasure than ever before.

Dancing is perhaps the most popular of all the early simple pleasures. Every frontier gathering becomes an occasion to dance, and the most sought-after person in every region is the man or woman who plays the fiddle.

More free time means the chance to spend precious hours away from the farm. And what better way to spend that time than at a horse race? Horse racing in America is as old as the nation itself, and nowhere is it more popular than on the frontier. Men and women who have spent countless hours raising their own horses and racing them against each other watch professional riders compete on true thoroughbreds. Throughout the frontier, pioneer families make "going to the races" one of their most important forms of entertainment.

The bicycle, in its modern form, is introduced to America at the great Philadelphia Centennial Exposition in 1876. By the 1880's a cycling craze sweeps the country, and bicycle races become part of the national scene. Many pioneer families find yet another spectacle to capture their attention.

The Glorious Fourth. That's what early Americans call the Fourth of July. In a nation that is still very young, celebrating the country's independence is a major event. For pioneer families who have carved their independence out of the wilderness, it is a most special day. There are parades, band concerts and endless series of patriotic ceremonies and speeches. At noon, families gather together for a giant picnic, and in the evening there is a community dance. Everywhere, from early morning to late in the night, there are fireworks.

Along with the Glorious Fourth, there is another eagerly awaited annual event. For three days in late September, the county fair captures the minds and hearts of pioneer families. They cheer at the ox-pulling contests, the horse races and the boxing and wrestling matches. Here most frontier families are introduced to inventions that will soon change their lives. Along with exhibitions of the latest farm machinery, men, women and children marvel at the displays of such modern miracles as the phonograph, the telephone and the electric light.

There is still another joy in going to the fair. The whole family gets the chance to show off. Father enters his prize animals in the livestock judging. Mother competes for a blue ribbon with her pies and preserves. Children proudly display the squashes and turnips they have grown.

In an age with no radio or movies or television, the county fair presents sights and sounds as different from the pioneer's everyday world as anything could be. Some of the attractions are truly spectacular.

There is also the circus. For many pioneer children and their parents, the circus is the biggest event of the year. "Each year," writes a former prairie farm boy, "the circus comes along from the East trailing clouds of glorified dust and filling our minds with the color of romance." The romance includes acrobats, clowns, elephants, tigers and brass bands. At the circus, frontier families hear the latest songs and laugh at jokes they'll retell all year long. "We always went home weary with excitement . . . but content," recalls another pioneer youngster. "Next day as we resumed work in the field, the memory [of the circus] went with us like a golden cloud."

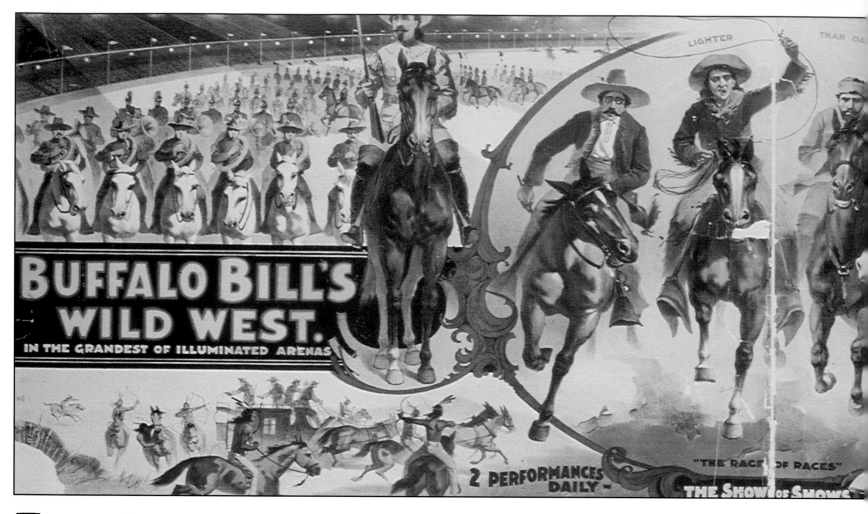

In 1883, William Cody organizes the Wild West Show, which he takes across the nation. Buffalo Bill, as he is called, is one of the most famous men in America. Stories—only some of them true—of his adventures as a buffalo hunter, Indian fighter, cavalry scout and pony express rider have been told for years throughout the frontier. The Wild West Show features scores of cowboys and cowgirls who display amazing skills at riding, roping and shooting. It presents equally skilled Native Americans. Audiences are treated to "historic" battles, most of which never really took place. The Wild West Show is a tremendous success. It becomes yet another attraction for pioneer families who are rapidly learning the joys of seeking pleasure.

Buffalo Bill's success leads to a host of imitators. More than fifty other Wild West Shows are formed. All present a romantic and exaggerated picture of frontier life. It is a portrayal that adds to the rapidly growing sentimentalized myth of life in the great West.

SCHOOLS AND TOWNS

As machinery increasingly provides time away from the farm, many pioneer families begin to realize one of their fondest dreams. Now they can send their children to school. The students still have many farm chores to complete. They are up as early as four A.M., milking the cows, hauling water and chopping wood before heading off to school.

The opening of a new frontier school is a major event. The first prairie schools were made of sod. Inside there is a single dirt-floored classroom where students of all ages are taught by one teacher. Subjects include history, arithmetic, agriculture, geography, spelling, reading, and grammar.

In some farm communities, larger schools are built with separate classrooms for students of different ages. Most pupils still walk long distances to school, but those lucky enough to live along the route of early school "buses" get to ride.

Most teachers are unmarried women. Some are not much older than their oldest students. To make up for their low pay, they "board out," living rent-free in the homes of their students, moving from home to home throughout the school year.

A good part of the pioneer family's new free time is spent in the town closest to the farm. The earliest towns are most often nothing more than a rough row of hastily-built wooden buildings with large signs. A town usually includes a horse stable, a post office, a hotel, at least one saloon and a general store. The prairie earth is the street, while nailed-together wooden planks serve as the sidewalk.

The general store is the most important building in the town. Here the settler buys everything from penny candy for the children to tools and kerosene lamps to flour, sugar and other packaged foods. When times get better, it is at the general store that Mother will buy her sewing machine and Father will purchase the latest shirt collars from back East, and here every member of the family has the chance to socialize with friends and neighbors.

The growth of frontier towns keeps pace with the huge increase in the number of settlers who pour into the West. In 1859, Denver, Colorado, is a tiny village. Many residents actually live in tents.

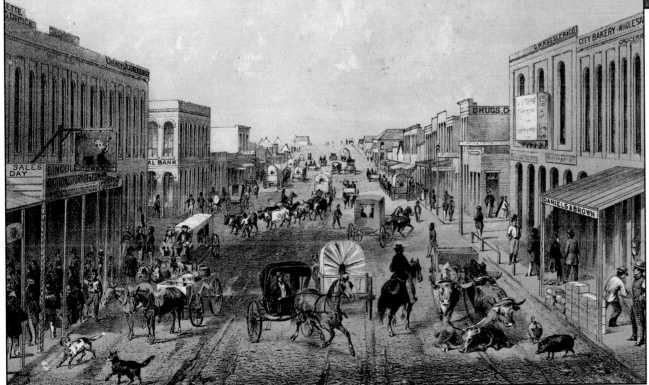

It takes Denver only seven years to grow into a bustling town complete with a bank, a bakery, a drugstore and all kinds of specialty shops.

The railroad plays an important role in the growth of the frontier towns. The places that grow most rapidly are those where the train stops, bringing both town settlers and the latest in goods for store owners to sell. Mason City, Iowa, is such a town. In 1870, it has a population of less than 700, and its main street looks like something right out of an early western movie. By the end of the 1890's, some 10,000 people live in Mason City, and its wooden Main Street buildings have been replaced by the most up-to-date brick structures.

By the 1890's, towns like Topeka, Kansas, and Des Moines, Iowa, have grown into cities. They boast such modern luxuries as electric lights, telephones, trolley cars and paved streets and sidewalks. Most of the pioneers have come to the West to avoid crowded city life, yet they celebrate what is being built. This seems like a contradiction, but the sight of full-fledged cities on the once-empty plains fills them with pride in all that has been accomplished.

AMERICA'S BREADBASKET

The prairie itself becomes a symbol of achievement as well. By the 1880's, it is covered with crops so thick and tall that people actually get lost walking through them. The pioneers have turned the prairie into the breadbasket of America.

As artists celebrate all that western farmers have accomplished, they focus not only on their crops but on the animals they have raised as well. In some of the paintings, the size of the animals is exaggerated. But the pioneer farmers have, in fact, produced extraordinary numbers of livestock. Like the crops they have grown, the cattle, sheep, pigs, and other animals they have raised will help feed not only America but other nations as well.

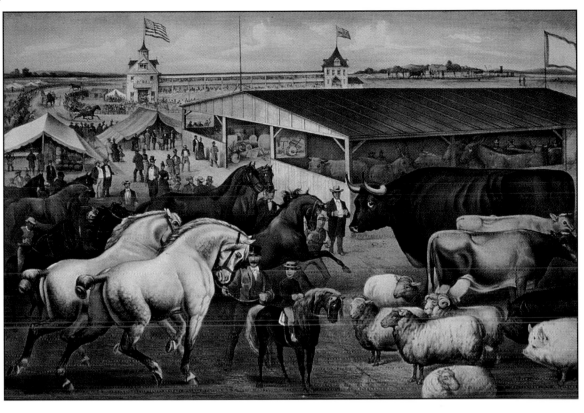

Photographers as well as artists join in the celebration. They capture pictures of extraordinary crops, such as potatoes bigger than boulders, which the pioneers have grown in the rich prairie soil.

The pioneers' way of life will always be challenging. They will always battle nature, and they will seldom get the prices they want for all they grow. But less than fifty years after the first settlers arrive on the plains, thousands of pioneers have replaced their sod houses with solid wood or brick homes. These homes are surrounded by the tall trees they have planted. By 1890, so much of the land has been settled that the government declares that the West is no longer a frontier. Many pioneers' dreams of a better life for themselves and their children have come true.

The pioneers have not only built better lives; they have built more than half a nation. No longer will the land they have come to be called the unsettled West or the Wild West. It will now be named the Great West. Prairie schooners, steamboats, trains, mountain men, miners, surveyors, lumberjacks, cowboys, merchants and farm families have all become part of one of America's greatest adventures.

THE GREAT WEST

History books will record the names of mountain men like Daniel Boone and Kit Carson, famous cowboys like Buffalo Bill, mythical lumberjacks like Paul Bunyan and even great western artists and photographers like George Catlin and William Henry Jackson. But the names of the ordinary people—the women, men and children who established permanent homes and farmed the land—will, for the most part, be lost to history. Yet is it these pioneers who are the real heroes of the great western adventure. They have proven that with courage and hard work, anything is possible. They have shown that no sacrifice is too great for those who follow a dream.

The Library of Congress

All of the photographs, lithographs, engravings, paintings, line drawings, posters, song lyrics, song-sheet covers, broadsides and other illustrative materials contained in this book have been culled from the collections of the Library of Congress. The Library houses the largest collection of stored knowledge on earth. Within its walls lie treasures that show us how much more than a "library" a great library can be.

The statistics that help define the Library are truly amazing. It has more books from America and England than anywhere else, yet barely one half of its collections are in English. It contains more maps, globes, charts and atlases than any other place on earth. It houses one of the largest collections of photographs in the world, the largest collection of films in America, almost every phonograph record ever made in the United States and the collections of the American Folklife Center. The Library also contains over six million volumes on hard sciences and applied technology.

It is a very modern institution as well. Dr. James Billington, the Librarian of Congress, has defined the Library's future through his vision of a "library without walls." "I see the Library of Congress in the future," he has said, "as an active catalyst for civilization, not just a passive mausoleum of cultural accomplishments of the past." A good example of this commitment is the Library's National Demonstration Laboratory, which, through hands-on work stations, offers over 200 examples of the latest innovations in interactive video and computer learning.

The Library of Congress was originally established to serve the members of Congress. Over the years it has evolved into a great national library. Unlike almost every other national library in the world, the Library of Congress does not limit the use of its collections to accredited scholars. Ours is a national library made by the people for the people, and is open to all the people. Fondly referred to as "the storehouse of the national memory," it is truly one of our proudest and most important possessions.

Index

Numbers in *italics* indicate photographs, maps, and illustrations.

trail drive, 47, *47*
storytelling of, 48, *48*
wranglers, 47
cowgirls, 44

Dakota gold strike, 21
dangers faced
    by pioneers in covered wagons, 32, *32*, 33,
        33
    by farmers, 57, 58, *58*
    by mountain men, 13, *13*
Deere, John, 53
Denver, Colorado, 79, *79*
Des Moines, Iowa, 81
dust storms, 57

"Emigrant Song," 41

Farmers/farming
    animals, 53, *53, 54*, 83, *83*
    clothing of, 55
    at county fair, 71, *71*, 72, *72*
    crops of, 11, *11*, 53, 65, *65*, 82, *82*, 83, *86*
    hardships of, 57, *57*, 58, *58*, 59, *59*
    harvest of, 55, *55*, 65, *65*, 67
    immigrants westward bound, 26, 42
    machinery, 64, *64*, 65, *65*, 66, *66, 67*
    New Englanders who go west, 26
    as pioneers, 8, 10, *10*, 11, *11*, 53, *53*, 56,
        56

plow, invention of, 53
women, 53, *54*, 55, *55*, 58, *59*, 62, *62*
work of, 53, *53*, 54, *54*, 55, *55*
    See also frontier family
flatboat, 37, *37*
food of first pioneers, 18
forests
    eastern, 17
    and lumberjacks, 49, *49*, 86
    northwest, 49
Fourth of July celebration, 70, *70*
free time/fun on the frontier, 67
    bicycling, 69, *69*
    children's play, 68
    circus, 73, *73*
    county fair, 71, *71*, 72, *72*
    dancing, 68
    family pastimes, 68
    Fourth of July celebration, 70, *70*
    horse racing, 69, *69*
    Wild West Show, 74, *74*, 75, *75*
frontier family, *2, 50, 51, 60*
    children in, 53, 54, *54*, 55, *55*, 56, *56*, 58
    clearing land, 17, *17*, 18, *18*
    courage of, 10
    farming life of, 53, *53*, 54, *54*, 55, *55*
    food of, 18
    free time/fun, 67, 68, *68*, 69, *69*, 70, *70*,
        73, *73*
    hardships of, 57, *57*, 58, *58*, 59, *59*
    homes of, *2,* 10, *18*, 52, *52*, 84, *84*
    importance of, 50
    relationships in, 56, *56*

size of, 54
frontier towns, 29, 43, 78, *78*, 79, *79*, 80, *81*
    general store in, 78, *78*
fur industry, 12, 14
fur trappers. *See* trappers

Garfield, James, 43
general store, 78, *78*
gold seekers, 8, 20, *20*, 21, *21*, 22
Great Plains
    beavers in, 13
    hunters and trappers in, 14, *14*
    Native Americans of, 14, *14*
    and Oregon Trail, 29, *29*
    river travel to, 37
    See also prairie
Great West, 85, *85*
guides and scouts, 15, *15*
Guthrie, Jr., A. B., 45

Homes, *10, 18,* 52, *52,* 84, *84*
"home stations," 36
horses, 31, 66
    and cowboys, 45, 46
    for mountain men, 13, *13*
    racing, 69, *69*
    for stagecoaches, 36
hunters, 8, 12, *12*, 13, *13*
    Native Americans as, 14, *14*
    See also mountain men
hunting, 18, *18*